The Kids' FUN-FILLED SEARCH & FIND BOOK

By
Tony Tallarico

kids books® Incorporated

FIND FREDDIE

WHERE ARE THEY?

F

Jake
ake
ke
e

FIND FREDDIE
AT HOME AND . . .

- [ ] Alligator
- [x] Apple
- [ ] Big foot
- [x] Bird's nest
- [x] Boxing glove
- [ ] Bug
- [ ] Cupcake
- [ ] Deflated balloon
- [x] Dinosaur
- [x] 4 Drumsticks
- [ ] Eight ball
- [ ] Electric guitar
- [x] False teeth
- [x] Fire hydrant
- [ ] Football helmet
- [ ] Footprints
- [x] Giant pencil
- [ ] "Goof Off" medal
- [x] 2 Hamburgers
- [ ] Lifesaver
- [x] 2 Locomotives
- [ ] Magnifying glass
- [x] Mailbox
- [x] Model plane
- [x] Monster hand
- [x] Mouse house
- [ ] 3 Music notes
- [ ] Paintbrush
- [ ] Ping-pong net
- [ ] "Quarantine"
- [ ] Sled
- [x] Slice of pizza
- [x] Snake
- [x] Soccer ball
- [ ] 3 Speakers
- [ ] Tent
- [ ] Thermometer
- [ ] "Think Small"
- [ ] 13:15
- [ ] Top hat
- [ ] Toy car
- [ ] Tricycle
- [ ] "Yech!"
- [ ] Yo-yo

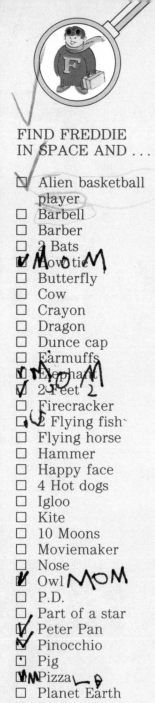

FIND FREDDIE IN SPACE AND . . .

- ☑ Alien basketball player
- ☐ Barbell
- ☐ Barber
- ☐ 3 Bats
- ☑ Bowtie
- ☐ Butterfly
- ☐ Cow
- ☐ Crayon
- ☐ Dragon
- ☐ Dunce cap
- ☐ Earmuffs
- ☑ Elephant
- ☑ 2 Feet 2
- ☐ Firecracker
- ☐ 2 Flying fish
- ☐ Flying horse
- ☐ Hammer
- ☐ Happy face
- ☐ 4 Hot dogs
- ☐ Igloo
- ☐ Kite
- ☐ 10 Moons
- ☐ Moviemaker
- ☐ Nose
- ☑ Owl
- ☐ P.D.
- ☐ Part of a star
- ☑ Peter Pan
- ☑ Pinocchio
- ☐ Pig
- ☑ Pizza
- ☐ Planet Earth
- ☐ Santa Claus
- ☐ Seal
- ☐ Skateboard
- ☐ Skull planet
- ☐ Space cat
- ☐ "Stairwars"
- ☐ Submarine
- ☐ Sunglasses
- ☐ Telescope
- ☐ Traffic signal
- ☐ Truck
- ☐ Tulips
- ☐ Two-headed alien

FIND FREDDIE AT SCHOOL AND...

- ☑ Apple
- ☐ Awakening monster
- ☐ Balloon
- ☐ "Ban Homework"
- ☐ Bare feet
- ☐ 2 Baseball bats
- ☐ Baton twirler
- ☐ Bowling ball
- ☐ Boy Scout
- ☐ Cake
- ☐ Cannon
- ☐ Clock setter
- ☐ Coach
- ☐ Cook
- ☐ "Disco"
- ☐ Explosion
- ☐ Fish tank
- ☐ Guitar
- ☐ Headless horseman
- ☐ Helium filled bubble gum
- ☐ Jump rope
- ☐ Lost ear
- ☐ Mouse attack
- ☐ Pumpkin
- ☐ 2 Rabbits
- ☐ 5 Report cards
- ☐ Roller skates
- ☐ Robot
- ☐ Rocket launch
- ☐ "Room To Let"
- ☐ 4 "School Closed" signs
- ☐ Secret trap door
- ☐ Ship
- ☐ 2 Sleeping students
- ☐ Snake
- ☐ Soccer practice
- ☐ Surfboard
- ☐ Tent
- ☐ Tuba
- ☐ 4 TV antennae
- ☐ Tyrannosaurus
- ☐ Water bomb
- ☐ Weightlifter

FIND FREDDIE
ON THE SCHOOL
BUS TRIP AND . . .

- ☐ Airplane
- ☐ Alligator
- ☐ Ambulance
- ☐ 5 Balloons
- ☐ Banana
- ☐ Barbershop
- ☐ Birdcage
- ☐ Boat
- ☐ "Bubble Gum Co."
- ☐ Burger-mobile
- ☐ Circus tent
- ☐ 3 Clocks
- ☐ Closed road
- ☐ Covered wagon
- ☐ Diver
- ☐ Doghouse
- ☐ Donkey
- ☐ Fish-mobile
- ☐ Garbage truck
- ☐ Gas station
- ☐ Ghost
- ☐ Horseshoe
- ☐ Hotel
- ☐ Igloo-mobile
- ☐ Jack-in-the-box
- ☐ Jellybean factory
- ☐ Lake serpent
- ☐ Library
- ☐ Locomotive
- ☐ 2 Mice
- ☐ Milk truck
- ☐ One-eyed monster
- ☐ Sailor cap
- ☐ Sandwich
- ☐ "72"
- ☑ 4 Sheep
- ☐ "Shopping Mall"
- ☐ 2 Skulls
- ☐ Sombrero
- ☐ Teepee-mobile
- ☐ Telephone
- ☐ Telescope
- ☐ Tennis racket
- ☐ Tow truck
- ☐ 2 Used tires

FIND FREDDIE IN MONSTERVILLE AND . . .

- [x] 6 Arrows
- [x] Bathbrush
- [x] 13 Bats
- [x] Ben Franklin
- [x] Broken clock
- [ ] Broken heart
- [ ] Carrot
- [ ] Clothespin
- [ ] Cowgirl
- [ ] Daisy
- [ ] "Dead End"
- [ ] Dog
- [ ] Eye in the sky
- [ ] Flying carpet
- [ ] Garbage can
- [ ] 6 Ghosts
- [ ] "Harvard Drop-Out"
- [x] Humpty Dumpty
- [x] Ice cream cone
- [ ] Key
- [ ] "Kids Ahead"
- [ ] Kite
- [x] Ladder
- [ ] Mailbox
- [ ] Mail carrier
- [ ] Ms. Transylvania
- [ ] "No Fishing"
- [x] 3 Number 13's
- [ ] One-eyed monster
- [ ] "One way"
- [ ] Octopus
- [ ] 7 Pumpkins
- [ ] Rabbit
- [ ] Skeleton
- [ ] 8 Skulls
- [ ] Sprinkler
- [ ] Tic-tac-toe
- [ ] Truck
- [ ] TV set
- [ ] Weird doctor
- [ ] 2 Welcome mats
- [ ] Window washer
- [ ] Witch
- [ ] Young Dracula's wagon

FIND FREDDIE AT THE AIRPORT AND . . .

- [ ] Arrow
- [x] Banana peel
- [x] 3 Bats
- [x] Bear
- [ ] Bird in love
- [ ] Boots
- [ ] Bride and groom
- [ ] Chicken
- [x] Clown
- [ ] Cow
- [ ] Dart
- [ ] Dog pilot
- [ ] "Don't Fly"
- [ ] "Fly"
- [ ] Flying saucer
- [x] 4 Fuel trucks
- [x] Globe
- [x] Golfer
- [ ] Hockey stick
- [ ] Horse
- [ ] "ICU2"
- [ ] Leaping lizard
- [x] Long beard
- [ ] Luggage carrier
- [ ] "One Way"
- [ ] 3 Paper planes
- [ ] Photographer
- [ ] Pterosaur
- [ ] Rabbit
- [ ] 2 Sailboats
- [x] Santa Claus
- [x] Seesaw
- [x] Sherlock Holmes
- [ ] Shooting star
- [ ] Space capsule
- [x] "Star Wreck"
- [ ] Super hero
- [ ] Telescope
- [x] Teepee
- [x] 2 Unicorns
- [ ] Walnut
- [ ] Watermelon slice
- [ ] Windsock
- [ ] Winged man
- [ ] Wooden leg

FIND FREDDIE AT THE BALLPARK AND . . .

- ☐ Basketball
- ☐ 3 Beach balls
- ☐ 3 Birds
- ☐ Bone
- ☐ Boxing glove
- ☐ Bubble gum bubble
- ☐ Car
- ☐ Clothesline
- ☐ Cyclist
- ☐ 3 Dancers
- ☐ Elephant
- ☐ Fish
- ☐ Football team
- ☐ Frankenstein monster
- ☐ Ghost
- ☐ Giraffe
- ☐ Gorilla
- ☐ "Happy Section"
- ☐ 3 Hearts
- ☐ Horse
- ☐ 2 "Hot" dogs
- ☐ Lawn mower
- ☐ Lost shoe
- ☐ Mascot
- ☐ Monster hand
- ☐ 6 "No. 1" hands
- ☐ "Out" banner
- ☐ Painter
- ☐ 5 Paper airplanes
- ☐ Parachutist
- ☐ Rabbit
- ☐ Showers
- ☐ Sleeping player
- ☐ Snowman
- ☐ Tic-tac-toe
- ☐ Torn pants
- ☐ Turtle
- ☐ 4 TV cameras
- ☐ 2 TV sets
- ☐ Two-gloved fan
- ☐ 3 Umbrellas
- ☐ Uncle Sam
- ☐ Viking
- ☐ Yellow slicker

FIND FREDDIE AT THE MUSEUM AND . . .

- ☐ 4 Artists
- ☐ Baby crying
- ☐ 3 Bees
- ☐ Bike racer
- ☐ Bomb
- ☐ Bowler
- ☐ Boy Scout
- ☐ Cactus
- ☐ Doctor
- ☐ Dracula
- ☐ Elephant
- ☐ Escaped convict
- ☐ Fire hose
- ☐ "First Prize"
- ☐ Girl fishing
- ☐ "For Sail"
- ☐ Giant soda
- ☐ Giant whistle
- ☐ Hamburger
- ☐ Hammock
- ☐ 5 Hearts
- ☐ Jester
- ☐ Juggler
- ☐ "Last Clean Air"
- ☐ Man rowing
- ☐ Mirror
- ☐ Mummy
- ☐ Musician
- ☐ Peanuts
- ☐ Peanut vendor
- ☐ Photographer
- ☐ Pizza delivery
- ☐ Princess
- ☐ Rope climber
- ☐ Sand castle
- ☐ Santa Claus
- ☐ Sherlock Holmes
- ☐ "Slowsand"
- ☐ Smoke signals
- ☐ Space capsule
- ☐ Sun
- ☐ Target
- ☐ Taxi
- ☐ Telephone booth
- ☐ "Thin Ice"

FIND FREDDIE IN THE OLD WEST TOWN AND . . .

- ☑ Alien
- ☐ Bald Indian
- ☐ Banana peel
- ☐ Bearded man
- ☐ 7 Bedbugs
- ☐ Boot Hill
- ☐ 6 Cactuses
- ☐ Cat
- ☐ "Condos"
- ☐ 5 Ducklings
- ☐ Fire hydrant
- ☐ Fistfight
- ☐ Flying saucer
- ☐ "Ghost Town"
- ☐ Hand-in-a-box
- ☐ Hobo hitchhiker
- ☐ Jailbreak
- ☐ Jockey
- ☐ Lasso
- ☐ Long johns
- ☐ One-man-band
- ☐ Painted mountain
- ☐ Parking meter
- ☐ Piano player
- ☐ Piggy bank
- ☐ 3 Rabbits
- ☐ Rain cloud
- ☐ Rhinoceros
- ☐ Rocking horse
- ☐ Satellite dish
- ☐ Shark fin
- ☐ Sharpshooter
- ☐ Sheriff
- ☐ Snake
- ☐ Snowman
- ☐ Soccer ball
- ☐ Stampede
- ☐ "Tacos"
- ☐ 8 Teepees
- ☐ "Texas"
- ☐ Theater
- ☐ 2 Tombstones
- ☐ Unicorn
- ☐ Witch

FIND FREDDIE

LOOK FOR LISA

HUNT FOR HECTOR

SEARCH FOR SAM

HUNT FOR HECTOR

WHERE ARE THEY?

HUNT FOR HECTOR
AT THE DOG HALL
OF FAME
AND . . .

- Alien
- Astronaut
- Automobile
- Babe Ruff
- 2 Birds
- Boot
- "Buffalo Bull"
- Cannon
- Cat
- "Cave Dog"
- Clown
- Cook
- Doghouse
- "Down Boy"
- Elephant
- Fallen star
- Flying dog
- Football
- Ghost dog
- 2 Giant bones
- Guard dog
- Hot dog
- Husky
- Indian
- Juggler
- Kangaroo
- Man on leash
- Mirror
- Moon
- Mouse
- Napoleon
- Photographer
- Pilgrim
- Pirate flag
- Record player
- Santa hound
- Sheep
- Sherlock Bones
- Stamp
- Super hero
- Super poodle
- Target
- Tin can
- Umpire

HUNT FOR HECTOR AT DOG SCHOOL AND . . .

- ☐ A-ARF
- ☐ Artist's model
- ☐ Banana peel
- ☐ Building plans
- ☐ Cat
- ☐ Chalk
- ☐ Clipboard
- ☐ Cloud
- ☐ Comic book
- ☐ Cook
- ☐ Cork
- ☐ Crown
- ☐ 2 Dancing dogs
- ☐ Doggy bag
- ☐ Doggy bank
- ☐ Dogwood
- ☐ Dunce cap
- ☐ Eraser
- ☐ Fire hydrant
- ☐ Flying bone
- ☐ 2 Forks
- ☐ Frankendog
- ☐ Genie
- ☐ Graduate
- ☐ Hammer
- ☐ Handkerchief
- ☐ "Hi, Mom!"
- ☐ "History Of Bones"
- ☐ Hockey stick
- ☐ "How To Bark"
- ☐ Leash
- ☐ Mail carrier
- ☐ Mush
- ☐ 2 Pencils
- ☐ P.T.A.
- ☐ Roller skates
- ☐ Saw
- ☐ 2 School bags
- ☐ Scooter
- ☐ Sun
- ☐ Sunglasses
- ☐ Triangle
- ☐ T-square

HUNT FOR HECTOR
AMONG THE DOG
CATCHERS
AND . . .

- ☑ Airplane
- ☐ Alien
- ☐ "Arf"
- ☐ Balloon
- ☐ Barber pole
- ☐ Carrots
- ☐ 5 Cats
- ☐ 3 Chimneys
- ☐ 3 Dog bowls
- ☐ 7 Dog catchers
- ☐ Doghouse
- ☐ Drums
- ☐ Firedogs
- ☐ 4 Fire hydrants
- ☐ Fisherdog
- ☐ 2 Flagpoles
- ☐ Flying saucer
- ☐ Gas mask
- ☐ 2 Howling dogs
- ☐ "Keep Things Clean"
- ☐ Mailbox
- ☐ Manhole cover
- ☐ 9 Police dogs
- ☐ 2 Restaurants
- ☐ Roadblock
- ☐ Rock and roll dog
- ☐ Santa dog
- ☐ Scout
- ☐ Shower
- ☐ Slice of pizza
- ☐ Streetlight
- ☐ 4 Super hero dogs
- ☐ Telephone
- ☐ Trail of money
- ☐ Trash can
- ☐ Tree
- ☐ 10 Trucks
- ☐ Turtle
- ☐ TV antenna
- ☐ TV camera
- ☐ Umbrella

HUNT FOR HECTOR
WHERE THE RICH
AND FAMOUS DOGS
LIVE AND . . .

HUNT FOR HECTOR AT THE K-9 CLEANUP AND . . .

- ☐ Anchor
- ☐ Bath brush
- ☐ 3 Birds
- ☐ Bomb
- ☐ Broom
- ☐ 2 Burned out light bulbs
- ☐ Cannon
- ☐ Cat
- ☐ Coffin
- ☐ Dog bowl
- ☐ Doghouse
- ☐ Dog in disguise
- ☐ Elephant
- ☐ 4 Empty food cans
- ☐ 3 Fire hydrants
- ☐ Fire pig
- ☐ Fisherdog
- ☐ Flying fish
- ☐ Frankenswine
- ☐ Garbage can
- ☐ Horse
- ☐ Indian dog
- ☐ "K-8"
- ☐ Life preserver
- ☐ Lunch box
- ☐ Mermaid
- ☐ Mob spy
- ☐ Mouse
- ☐ Net
- ☐ Oil leak
- ☐ Old dog
- ☐ Old tire
- ☐ Palm tree
- ☐ Penguin
- ☐ Periscope
- ☐ Pighole cover
- ☐ Rabbit
- ☐ Rubber duck
- ☐ Sailor pig
- ☐ Skateboard
- ☐ Telescope
- ☐ Violin case

HUNT FOR HECTOR
AT THE SUPER
DOG BOWL
AND . . .

- ☑ "Almost
    Wet Paint"
- ☑ Arrow
- ☑ Beach ball
- ☑ Bird
- ☑ Bowling ball
- ☐ Cactus
- ☐ Candycane
- ☑ Cheerleaders
- ☑ Chicken
- ☑ Coach
- ☐ "Dog Aid"
- ☐ "Dogs U"
- ☐ Egg
- ☐ "Exit"
- ☐ 3 Flowers
- ☐ Ghost
- ☐ Heart
- ☐ Hobby horse
- ☐ Hot dog
- ☑ Megaphone
- ☐ "Mom"
- ☐ Mouse
- ☐ "No Barking"
- ☐ "Number 1"
- ☐ Paddleball
- ☐ Paintbrush
- ☐ 2 Pigs
- ☐ Pirate
- ☐ Propeller cap
- ☑ 5 Pumpkins
- ☐ Rabbit
- ☐ Skull and
    crossbones
- ☐ Super Bowl I
- ☐ Super Bowl II
- ☐ Super Bowl III
- ☐ Sword
- ☐ Tombstone
- ☐ Turtle
- ☐ TV camera
- ☐ TV set
- ☐ Water bucket
- ☐ "Wet Paint"
- ☐ Worm

HUNT FOR HECTOR
AT THE DOG MALL
AND . . .

- ☐ Ball
- ☐ Balloon
- ☐ Barber shop
- ☐ Bat
- ☐ Bird's house
- ☐ Candle
- ☐ Candy cane
- ☐ 2 Cats
- ☐ Cheerleader
- ☐ Clown
- ☐ 2 Cookies
- ☐ Cup
- ☐ Dog bowls "Sale"
- ☐ Dog cake
- ☐ Doghouse
- ☐ Fish
- ☐ Flamingo
- ☐ Ghost
- ☐ Headphones
- ☐ Heart
- ☐ Helmet
- ☐ Howling Dog
- ☐ Human
- ☐ Ice cream cone
- ☐ Knight in armor
- ☐ Lollipop
- ☐ Mask
- ☐ Mouse
- ☐ Newsdog
- ☐ Newspaper reader
- ☐ Nut
- ☐ Paper airplane
- ☐ Pelican
- ☐ Pizza slice
- ☐ Police dog
- ☐ Pumpkin
- ☐ Scarf
- ☐ Stool
- ☐ Sunglasses
- ☐ Tennis racket
- ☐ Tire
- ☐ 2 Trash baskets
- ☐ Trophy
- ☐ Waiter

HUNT FOR HECTOR AT THE DOG OLYMPICS AND . . .

- ☐ Archer
- ☐ 7 Arrows
- ☐ Basketball
- ☐ Batter
- ☐ Bomb
- ☐ Bone balloon
- ☐ Boomerang
- ☐ Broom
- ☐ Caddy
- ☐ Car chase
- ☐ Cyclers
- ☐ Dunce cap
- ☐ Fencers
- ☐ "Fetch"
- ☐ Football
- ☐ "Go Dogs"
- ☐ Golf ball
- ☐ Gymnasts
- ☐ "Hi, Mom"
- ☐ Hockey game
- ☐ Horse
- ☐ Horseshoe
- ☐ Ice cream cone
- ☐ Karate chop
- ☐ Lacrosse stick
- ☐ Paper plane
- ☐ Pole vaulter
- ☐ Rower
- ☐ Skateboard
- ☐ Skier
- ☐ 2 Sleeping dogs
- ☐ Snow dog
- ☐ Soccer ball
- ☐ Starter's gun
- ☐ "Stop"
- ☐ Target
- ☐ Trainer
- ☐ TV camera
- ☐ "Very Thin Ice"
- ☐ Weight lifter
- ☐ Yo-yo

HUNT FOR HECTOR
AT THE TV QUIZ
SHOW
AND . . .

HUNT FOR HECTOR IN SPACE AND . . .

- ☐ Bark Vader
- ☐ Boat
- ☐ Boney Way
- ☐ Book
- ☐ Bow-wow land
- ☐ Boxing glove
- ☐ Cat
- ☐ Condo
- ☐ Dog catcher
- ☐ Dog graduate
- ☐ Dog trek
- ☐ Doggy bag
- ☐ Duck Rogers
- ☐ Emergency stop
- ☐ Fire hydrant
- ☐ Flying dog house
- ☐ Flying food dish
- ☐ Jail
- ☐ Kite
- ☐ Launch site
- ☐ Lost and found
- ☐ Mail carrier
- ☐ Map
- ☐ Moon dog
- ☐ "No Barking"
- ☐ Parachute
- ☐ Pirate
- ☐ Pizza
- ☐ Planet of the bones
- ☐ Planet of the dogs
- ☐ Police dog
- ☐ Pup tent
- ☐ Puppy trainer
- ☐ Robot dog
- ☐ Sleeping dog
- ☐ Space circus
- ☐ Surfboard
- ☐ Swimming pool
- ☐ Tire
- ☐ Unicycle
- ☐ Vampire dog
- ☐ Vanishing dog

HUNT FOR HECTOR IN DOGTOWN AND . . .

- ☐ "The Arf Building"
- ☐ Barbecue
- ☐ Bird bath
- ☐ Boat
- ☐ Bone crop
- ☐ Bookstore
- ☐ 2 Broken clocks
- ☐ 8 Broken windows
- ☐ 2 Cats
- ☐ "Curb Your Human"
- ☐ Dance studio
- ☐ 5 Fire hydrants
- ☐ Flag
- ☐ "For Rent"
- ☐ Fountain
- ☐ "Frozen Dog Food"
- ☐ Gas station
- ☐ "Happy Dog Mush"
- ☐ 3 Hard hats
- ☐ Ice cream truck
- ☐ Jogger
- ☐ Lawn mower
- ☐ Mail carrier
- ☐ Mechanic
- ☐ Motorcycle
- ☐ Movie theater
- ☐ Newsdog
- ☐ "People Catcher"
- ☐ Piano
- ☐ Pool
- ☐ Santa Claus
- ☐ Sleigh
- ☐ Sock
- ☐ Video shop
- ☐ Wagon
- ☐ Water tower
- ☐ Weather vane
- ☐ Window washer

HUNT FOR HECTOR   SEARCH FOR SAM   FIND FREDDIE   LOOK FOR LISA

LOOK FOR LISA

WHERE ARE THEY?

LOOK FOR LISA AT THE MARATHON AND . . .

- ☐ Alien
- ☐ Alligator
- ☐ Ape
- ☐ Astronaut
- ☐ 2 Banana peels
- ☐ Barbell
- ☐ 5 Bats
- ☐ Big nose
- ☐ Cable car
- ☐ Cake
- ☐ Caveman
- ☐ 8 Chimneys
- ☐ Clown
- ☐ Convict
- ☐ Deep sea diver
- ☐ Drummer
- ☐ 2 Elephants
- ☐ Fire fighter
- ☐ Fish
- ☐ Flying carpet
- ☐ Football player
- ☐ Frankenstein monster
- ☐ Horse
- ☐ Ice skater
- ☐ Long-haired lady
- ☐ Man in a barrel
- ☐ Moose head
- ☐ Octopus
- ☐ Pig
- ☐ 6 Quitters
- ☐ Santa Claus
- ☐ Skier
- ☐ Sleeping jogger
- ☐ Snow White
- ☐ Tuba
- ☐ 2 Turtles
- ☐ Vampire
- ☐ Viking
- ☐ Waiter
- ☐ Worm

LOOK FOR LISA
AFTER SCHOOL
AND . . .

- ☐ Airplane
- ☐ 2 Aliens
- ☐ Beanie
  with propeller
- ☐ Beard
- ☐ Blackboard
- ☐ Books on wheels
- ☐ Bucket
- ☐ Bus driver
- ☐ "Class brain"
- ☐ Clown
- ☐ Coach
- ☐ Dog
- ☐ Fire hydrant
- ☐ Football player
- ☐ Ghost
- ☐ Hockey player
- ☐ "Junior"
- ☐ Man trapped
  in a book
- ☐ 3 Mice
- ☐ Monkey
- ☐ Periscope
- ☐ Photographer
- ☐ Piano player
- ☐ Pillow
- ☐ "P.U."
- ☐ Pumpkin
- ☐ Radio
- ☐ Sailor
- ☐ School mascot
- ☐ Scooter
- ☐ Shopping cart
- ☐ Skateboard
- ☐ Ski jumper
- ☐ Socks
- ☐ Sports car
- ☐ Sunglasses
- ☐ Tepee
- ☐ Top hat
- ☐ Trash basket
- ☐ Unicorn
- ☐ Wagon

LOOK FOR LISA AT THE ROCK CONCERT AND . . .

- ☐ Alligator
- ☐ Apple
- ☐ Artist
- ☐ Beans
- ☐ Clown
- ☐ 2 Dogs
- ☐ Dwarf
- ☐ "Empty TV"
- ☐ Farmer
- ☐ Football player
- ☐ 4 Ghosts
- ☐ Giraffe
- ☐ 3 Guitars
- ☐ Heart
- ☐ 2 Hippos
- ☐ Hot dogs
- ☐ Hot foot
- ☐ Jogger
- ☐ Lamppost
- ☐ Lost balloon
- ☐ Magician
- ☐ "No Bus Stop"
- ☐ Pig
- ☐ Pink flamingo
- ☐ Pizza delivery
- ☐ Real cross wind
- ☐ Record albums
- ☐ Robot
- ☐ Rock
- ☐ Rock queen
- ☐ Roll
- ☐ Rooster
- ☐ Scarecrow
- ☐ School bus
- ☐ Skateboard
- ☐ 15 Speakers
- ☐ Stars
- ☐ Tent
- ☐ "Too Heavy Metal"
- ☐ Turtle
- ☐ Witch
- ☐ Zebra

LOOK FOR LISA
ON THE FARM
AND . . .

LOOK FOR LISA AT THE BEACH AND . . .

- ☐ Artist
- ☐ Barrel of pickles
- ☐ Birdbath
- ☐ Boot
- ☐ 3 Bottles with notes
- ☐ Bubble gum
- ☐ 4 Cactuses
- ☐ 2 Clowns
- ☐ Cow
- ☐ Crocodile
- ☐ Dart thrower
- ☐ 4 Flying fish
- ☐ Hammerhead shark
- ☐ Leaking boat
- ☐ Lifesaver
- ☐ Litterbug
- ☐ Lost bathing suit
- ☐ 3 Mermaids
- ☐ Motorcyclist
- ☐ Mummy
- ☐ Musician
- ☐ Oil rig
- ☐ Pirate ship
- ☐ Polluted area
- ☐ 3 Radios
- ☐ Robinson Crusoe
- ☐ Rowboat
- ☐ Sailfish
- ☐ Seahorse
- ☐ Sea serpent
- ☐ Sleeping man
- ☐ Skull cave
- ☐ Stingray
- ☐ Submarine
- ☐ 6 Surfboards
- ☐ Telescope
- ☐ Thief
- ☐ Tricyclist
- ☐ Very quick sand
- ☐ 2 Water skiers

LOOK FOR LISA AT THE BIG SALE AND . . .

LOOK FOR LISA AROUND THE WORLD AND . . .

- ☑ Bear
- ☑ Big foot
- ☐ 2 Bridge builders
- ☐ Cactus
- ☐ Camel
- ☐ Cowboy
- ☐ Cup of coffee
- ☑ Cup of tea
- ☑ Dog
- ☑ Eskimo
- ☑ 12 Fish
- ☑ 2 Flying saucers
- ☐ Golfer
- ☐ Heart
- ☐ Ice castle
- ☐ Igloo
- ☐ Kangaroo
- ☐ Lighthouse
- ☐ Lion
- ☐ Mermaid
- ☐ Merman
- ☐ Oil well
- ☐ Ox
- ☐ 6 Penguins
- ☐ Rock singer
- ☐ 4 Sailboats
- ☐ Sea serpent
- ☐ 4 Skiers
- ☐ 2 Snowmen
- ☐ Stuck ship
- ☐ Submarine
- ☐ 3 Surfers
- ☐ Telescope
- ☐ 6 "Travel Agent" signs
- ☐ Tug boat
- ☐ T.V. set
- ☐ Unicorns in Utah
- ☐ Viking ship
- ☐ Walrus
- ☐ Whale

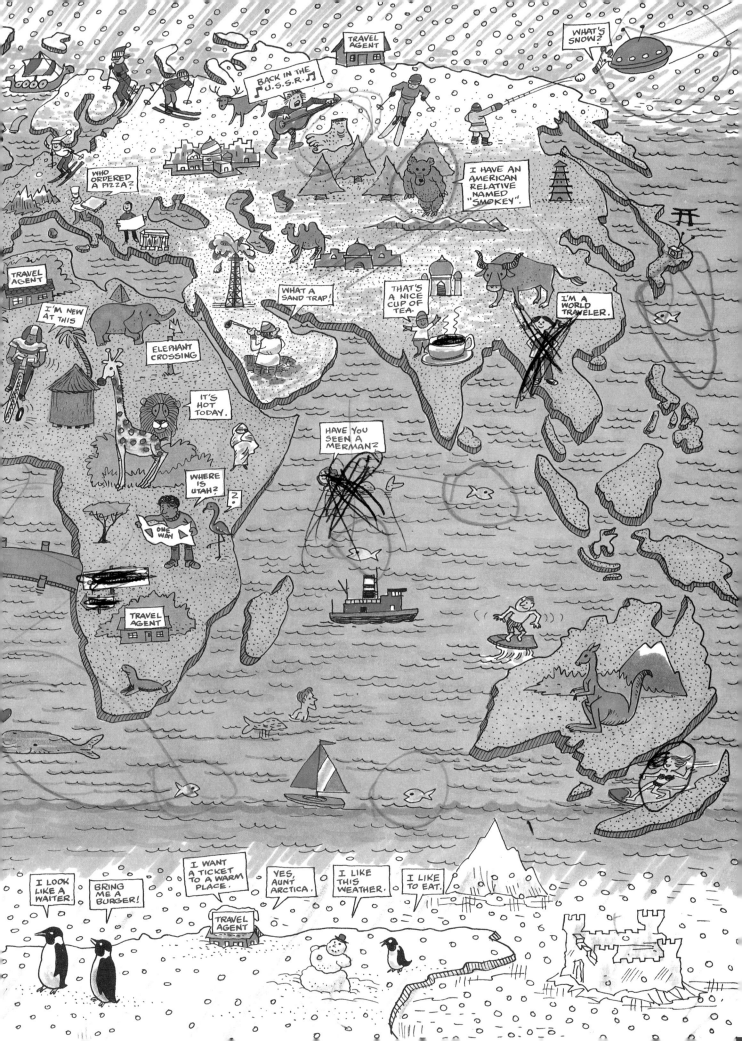

LOOK FOR LISA
AT THE LIBRARY
AND . . .

LOOK FOR LISA
AT THE
AMUSEMENT PARK
AND . . .

- ☐ Astronaut
- ☐ 15 Balloons
- ☐ Baseball
- ☐ Bomb
- ☐ Cactus
- ☐ Cheese
- ☐ Diplodocus
- ☐ "Do Not Read This"
- ☐ Entrance
- ☐ Exit
- ☐ Fishing hole
- ☐ 5 Ghosts
- ☐ Gorilla
- ☐ Graduate
- ☐ Headless man
- ☐ High diver
- ☐ Horse
- ☐ "Hot Dogs"
- ☐ "House Of Horrors"
- ☐ "Kisses"
- ☐ "Low Tide"
- ☐ 4 Mice
- ☐ 3 Monsters
- ☐ Mummy
- ☐ "No U-Turns"
- ☐ Pear
- ☐ Rocket
- ☐ Santa Claus
- ☐ "Scrambled Eggs"
- ☐ Skateboard
- ☐ Skull
- ☐ Snowman
- ☐ Thirteen o'clock
- ☐ Trash can
- ☐ Umbrella
- ☐ Vampire
- ☐ Witch

LOOK FOR LISA AT THE FLEA MARKET AND . . .

- ☐ Ape
- ☐ Bag of peanuts
- ☐ Baseball cards
- ☐ Bathtub
- ☐ Bicycle
- ☐ 2 Bird cages
- ☐ Box of records
- ☐ 2 Cactuses
- ☐ Candle
- ☐ Clown doll
- ☐ Cowboy
- ☐ 2 Dogs
- ☐ Duck
- ☐ 3 Fish
- ☐ Flower
- ☐ Football
- ☐ 2 Frogs
- ☐ Garbage basket
- ☐ Gas mask
- ☐ Giant shoe
- ☐ Graduate
- ☐ Hammer
- ☐ Knight in armor
- ☐ Lamp shade
- ☐ Man in bottle
- ☐ 2 Men with fleas
- ☐ Monster hand
- ☐ Pearl necklace
- ☐ Piggy bank
- ☐ Potted palm plant
- ☐ Rocking chair
- ☐ Saddle
- ☐ Scoutmaster
- ☐ Smoke signals
- ☐ Spinning wheel
- ☐ Sunglasses
- ☐ Tennis racket
- ☐ Toy locomotive
- ☐ Trumpet
- ☐ Yo-yo

LOOK FOR LISA
AS THE CIRCUS
COMES TO TOWN
AND . . .

- [ ] Ape
- [ ] Baby carriage
- [ ] 6 Balloons
- [ ] 2 Batons
- [ ] Bird
- [ ] Cactus
- [ ] Camel
- [ ] Candle
- [ ] Cannon
- [ ] Cat
- [ ] 13 Clowns
- [ ] 8 Dogs
- [ ] 5 Elephants
- [ ] "Exit"
- [ ] "For Rent"
- [ ] Giraffe
- [ ] 5 Happy faces
- [ ] 2 Indians
- [ ] Jack-in-the-box
- [ ] 2 Keystone cops
- [ ] Lion
- [ ] 2 Martians
- [ ] "Not Wet Paint"
- [ ] Rabbit
- [ ] Super hero
- [ ] 7 Tents
- [ ] Ticket seller
- [ ] Tightrope walker
- [ ] Tin man
- [ ] Top hat
- [ ] Turtle
- [ ] 3 Umbrellas
- [ ] Unicycle
- [ ] Weightlifter
- [ ] Witch

LOOK FOR LISA   FIND FREDDIE   SEARCH FOR SAM   HUNT FOR HECTOR

SEARCH FOR SAM
IN CAT CITY AND . . .

SEARCH FOR SAM
ON FRIDAY THE
13TH AND . . .

- Apple
- Ax
- Balloon
- 7 Bats
- 4 Black cats
- Bomb
- Candy cane
- Chicken
- Coffin
- Condos
- Cow
- Football
- "Ghost Office"
- 6 Ghosts
- Heart
- "Helping Hand"
- Junior vampire
- Kite eater
- Mad doctor
- Mailbox
- Man's head
- Mirror
- Mouse
- "No Screaming"
- Paint bucket
- Pirate
- 13 Pumpkins
- Quicksand
- Rabbit
- Ship
- Shovel
- Skull
- Snake
- 13 "13s"
- Trunk
- Turtle
- TV set
- Two-headed
  monster
- Vampire

SEARCH FOR SAM AT THE FAT CAT HEALTH CLUB AND . . .

SEARCH FOR SAM AT THE MIDNIGHT MEOWING AND . . .

SEARCH FOR SAM AT THE DISCO AND . . .

SEARCH FOR SAM
AT THE BATTLE
OF CATS AND
MICE AND . . .

- ☐ Banana peel
- ☐ Baseball
- ☐ Big cheese
- ☐ "Catnip"
- ☐ Catapult
- ☐ Cheese donut
- ☐ Chimney mouse
- ☐ Clock
- ☐ Condo
- ☐ 2 Cream pies
- ☐ Cup
- ☐ Dog
- ☐ Drummer
- ☐ Fake mouse
- ☐ 3 Fish
- ☐ Flower
- ☐ 'Fraidy cat
- ☐ Frankencat
- ☐ 4 Hearts
- ☐ Hobby horse
- ☐ Horn blower
- ☐ Hose
- ☐ Ink
- ☐ Judge
- ☐ Key
- ☐ Knapsack
- ☐ Light bulb
- ☐ Mask
- ☐ Monkey
- ☐ Mouse trap
- ☐ Owl
- ☐ 2 Pigs
- ☐ Quill pen
- ☐ Sleeping mouse
- ☐ Spider
- ☐ Sword
- ☐ Top hat
- ☐ Watering can
- ☐ Worm
- ☐ Yarn

SEARCH FOR SAM IN ANCIENT EGYPT AND . . .

- ☐ Accident victim
- ☐ 2 Alley cats
- ☐ Bandit
- ☐ 4 Birds
- ☐ 4 Camels
- ☐ Cat kite
- ☐ "Catnip"
- ☐ Catopatra
- ☐ Crocodile
- ☐ Dog
- ☐ Dog house
- ☐ 2 Elephants
- ☐ 2 Falling coconuts
- ☐ Fan
- ☐ 3 Fish
- ☐ Flower
- ☐ Flying carpet
- ☐ Garage
- ☐ Happy face
- ☐ Hippo
- ☐ Hot sand
- ☐ Jester
- ☐ Ladder
- ☐ 6 Mice
- ☐ Mummy
- ☐ Oasis
- ☐ 8 Pyramids
- ☐ Quicksand
- ☐ Sculptor
- ☐ Slow sand
- ☐ Snake-in-the-grass
- ☐ Snake-in-the-sand
- ☐ Snowman
- ☐ 5 Spears
- ☐ Sunglasses
- ☐ Surfer
- ☐ Taxi
- ☐ Telephone
- ☐ TV antenna
- ☐ Umbrella

VP CAT

SEARCH FOR SAM
AT THE CAT SHOW
AND . . .

- ☐ Banjo
- ☐ Beach chair
- ☐ Bird
- ☐ Black cat
- ☐ Cat costume
- ☐ Cat guard
- ☐ Cat in a hat
- ☐ Cat on a
  woman's head
- ☐ Clown
- ☐ Cow
- ☐ Curtain
- ☐ 2 Dogs
- ☐ Elephant
- ☐ Fat cat
- ☐ 2 Fish bowls
- ☐ Fishing pole
- ☐ Groucho cat
- ☐ Hobo cat
- ☐ Jogging cat
- ☐ 3 Judges
- ☐ Light bulb
- ☐ Lion
- ☐ "Moo Juice"
- ☐ Mouse
- ☐ Photographer
- ☐ Pizza
- ☐ Pool
- ☐ "Princess"
- ☐ Scaredy cat
- ☐ Scarf
- ☐ Scratching
  post
- ☐ Sombrero
- ☐ Sunglasses
- ☐ Telescope
- ☐ "The Real
  1st Prize"
- ☐ Tombstone
- ☐ Trombone
- ☐ "Wanted" poster
- ☐ Witch

SEARCH FOR SAM
WITH THE
DOGBUSTERS
AND . . .

- ☐ "Bark 1-642"
- ☐ "Baseball
  Cards"
- ☐ Binoculars
- ☐ Bird
- ☐ Boat
- ☐ "Brooklyn"
- ☐ Blimp
- ☐ Bomb
- ☐ Cage
- ☐ Clown
- ☐ Crash
- ☐ Crocodile
- ☐ Dog house
- ☐ Fire hydrant
- ☐ Fish tank
- ☐ Happy face
- ☐ Helicopter
- ☐ "Hideout
  For Rent"
- ☐ Hockey stick
- ☐ Horse
- ☐ Manhole
- ☐ Monster
- ☐ 2 Mice
- ☐ Net
- ☐ Periscope
- ☐ "Pizza"
- ☐ "Poison Ivy"
- ☐ Pumpkin
- ☐ "Quiet"
- ☐ Rabbit
- ☐ Robot
- ☐ Rope ladder
- ☐ Saddle
- ☐ Super hero
- ☐ Surfer
- ☐ Tank
- ☐ Taxi
- ☐ Tent
- ☐ Truck
- ☐ Used tire
- ☐ Witch

SEARCH FOR SAM AT THE NORTH POLE AND . . .

- ☑ Ball
- ☐ Bear
- ☐ 2 Birds
- ☐ 3 Candles
- ☑ 6 Candy canes
- ☐ Coal
- ☐ Drum
- ☐ Duck
- ☑ Fallen skater
- ☐ Fishing
- ☑ 2 Fires
- ☐ Globe
- ☐ Gloves
- ☐ Hammer
- ☑ Jack-in-the-box
- ☐ Kitty bank
- ☐ Lollypop
- ☐ Mailbox
- ☐ Miner
- ☑ "North Pole"
- ☐ Pie
- ☑ Pumpkin
- ☐ Rabbit
- ☐ Rocking horse
- ☐ Roller skater
- ☐ Skier
- ☑ Sleeping cat
- ☐ Sleeping mouse
- ☑ 3 Sleds
- ☐ Snowball thrower
- ☐ Star
- ☐ 2 Stockings
- ☑ Toy soldier
- ☐ Tree ornament
- ☐ Turtle
- ☐ T.V. antenna
- ☐ Wheelbarrow
- ☐ Wrapping paper
- ☐ 2 Wreaths
- ☑ 2 Zebras

SEARCH FOR SAM   FIND FREDDIE   HUNT FOR HECTOR   LOOK FOR LISA

WHERE ARE THEY?

DETECT DONALD

It was a dark and rainy night in Hollywood. Detective Donald had stopped to eat at his favorite diner.

DETECT DONALD AT THE CHEEZ-E DINER AND...

- [x] Arrow
- [ ] Bat
- [ ] Bird
- [x] Bow ties (3)
- [ ] Bowling ball
- [ ] Cactus
- [ ] Convict
- [ ] Cook
- [ ] Crown
- [ ] Dracula
- [ ] Dragon
- [ ] Eyeglasses (3)
- [ ] Fish
- [ ] Genie
- [ ] Ghost
- [ ] Guitar
- [ ] Heart
- [ ] Humpty Dumpty
- [ ] Jack-o'-lantern
- [ ] Mouse
- [ ] Pirate
- [ ] Rabbit
- [ ] Skull
- [ ] Stars (3)
- [ ] Super heroes
- [ ] Top hat
- [ ] Two-headed man
- [ ] Waitresses (2)
- [ ] Witch
- [ ] Wristwatch

When he stepped outside, he detected something strange going on. First he saw a large group of strange characters. Then....

...Detective Donald almost got run over by a horse and carriage! There were no cars or buses and people were wearing wigs and funny hats. Detective Donald thought he saw George Washington—but it couldn't be! He decided to investigate to find out what was going on.

DETECT DONALD IN COLONIAL AMERICA AND...

- ☐ Antenna
- ☐ Baseball
- ☐ Basket
- ☐ Bell
- ☐ Ben Franklin
- ☐ Betsy Ross
- ☐ Bone
- ☐ Broom
- ☐ Bucket
- ☐ Candles (2)
- ☐ Cannonballs (4)
- ☐ Cats (2)
- ☐ Chicken
- ☐ Clock
- ☐ Dogs (2)
- ☐ Drums (3)
- ☐ Duck
- ☐ Ear of corn
- ☐ Flower vase
- ☐ Horses (4)
- ☐ Kites (2)
- ☐ Lamppost
- ☐ Mouse
- ☐ One dollar bill
- ☐ Saw
- ☐ Shopping bag
- ☐ Spinning wheel
- ☐ TV set
- ☐ Wagons (2)
- ☐ Watering can

Suddenly, two knights on horseback carrying long lances went charging by. A king, queen, knights and maidens were watching a jousting tournament. *Where was he now?* wondered Detective Donald.

DETECT DONALD IN THE MIDDLE AGES AND...

- ☐ Alligator
- ☐ Balloons (2)
- ☐ Birds (2)
- ☐ Candy cane
- ☐ Dog
- ☐ Doorbell
- ☐ Fan
- ☐ Fish
- ☐ Hot dog
- ☐ Ice-cream cone
- ☐ Jack-o'-lantern
- ☐ Jester
- ☐ King
- ☐ Kite
- ☐ Musician
- ☐ Periscope
- ☐ Pig
- ☐ Pot
- ☐ Robin Hood
- ☐ Rose
- ☐ Santa Claus
- ☐ Skull
- ☐ Sock
- ☐ Stars (2)
- ☐ Target
- ☐ Toast
- ☐ Umpire
- ☐ Unicorn
- ☐ Vendor
- ☐ Wizard

After watching the tournament for awhile, Detective Donald walked through the castle...

...and into a room filled with laughter! There were lots of cartoon characters acting silly all around him. Things were getting stranger and stranger.

DETECT DONALD IN CARTOONLAND AND...

- ☐ Balloon
- ☐ Banana peel
- ☐ Baseball
- ☐ Beehive
- ☐ Book
- ☐ Brush
- ☐ Cars (2)
- ☐ Cheese
- ☐ Clothesline
- ☐ Fire hydrant
- ☐ Fish (2)
- ☐ Fishing pole
- ☐ Flower
- ☐ Ghost
- ☐ Golf club
- ☐ Hose
- ☐ Ice-cream cone
- ☐ Magnifying glass
- ☐ Net
- ☐ Owl
- ☐ Sandwich
- ☐ Soap
- ☐ Star
- ☐ Sunglasses (2)
- ☐ Super dude
- ☐ Train engine
- ☐ Turtle
- ☐ TV set
- ☐ Umbrella

As Detective Donald walked through a hole in the wall, he heard...

...“Ahoy mates, a landlubber!” It was a pirate ship, and pirates were dashing about with swords doing battle with anyone and everyone.

DETECT DONALD AT THE PIRATES' BATTLE AND...

- [ ] Basketball
- [ ] Birds (3)
- [ ] Broom
- [ ] Candle
- [ ] Cannonballs (4)
- [ ] Captain Hook
- [ ] Cat
- [ ] Cup
- [ ] Duck
- [ ] Fish
- [ ] Football
- [ ] Guitar
- [ ] Half moon
- [ ] Headless horseman
- [ ] Hearts (2)
- [ ] Hot dog
- [ ] Jack-o'-lantern
- [ ] Knight
- [ ] Mice (7)
- [ ] Mirror
- [ ] Piano
- [ ] Rooster
- [ ] Sailboat
- [ ] Snake
- [ ] Top hat
- [ ] Treasure chest
- [ ] Turtles (3)
- [ ] Watering can
- [ ] Wooden legs (3)
- [ ] Yellow brick road

Detective Donald thought it best to quickly move on.

What was happening? Detective Donald's surroundings began to change before his very eyes! Strange buildings and bizarre creatures replaced the pirates.

DETECT DONALD IN THE WORLD OF THE FUTURE AND...

- ☐ Baby carriage
- ☐ Bat
- ☐ Bottle
- ☐ Bow
- ☐ Clothespin
- ☐ Dog
- ☐ Flat tire
- ☐ Hammer
- ☐ Key
- ☐ Kite
- ☐ Ladder
- ☐ Little red riding creature
- ☐ Mailbox
- ☐ Parachute
- ☐ Pencil
- ☐ Phonograph record
- ☐ Pocket watch
- ☐ Red wagon
- ☐ Submarine sandwich
- ☐ Schoolbag
- ☐ Sled
- ☐ Snowman
- ☐ Straw
- ☐ Teeth
- ☐ Tree
- ☐ Two-headed creature
- ☐ Tepee
- ☐ Vacuum cleaner
- ☐ Witch

Out an exit he went, and into...

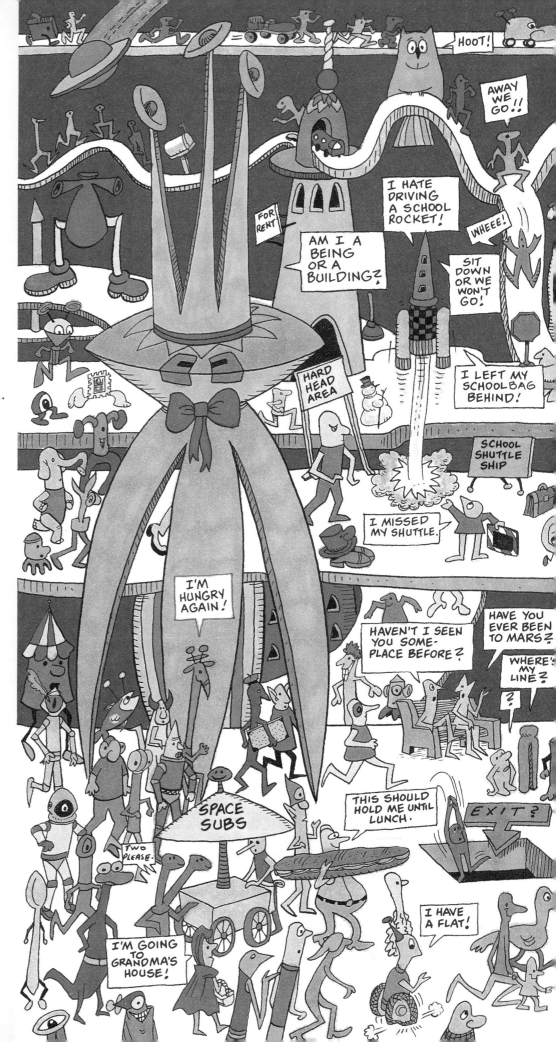

...French history a few hundred years ago. He was more confused than ever. Maybe I'm just having a weird dream, he thought.

DETECT DONALD IN NAPOLEON'S FRANCE AND...

- ☑ Alligator
- ☑ Axe
- ☑ Ballerina
- ☐ Balloon
- ☐ Baker
- ☐ Bell
- ☐ Cake
- ☐ Cannon
- ☐ Dracula
- ☐ Dragon
- ☐ Duck
- ☐ Eight ball
- ☐ Firecracker
- ☐ Flower
- ☐ French poodle
- ☐ King Kong
- ☐ Medals (2)
- ☐ Mermaid
- ☐ Movie camera
- ☐ Mummy
- ☐ Old tire
- ☐ One-eyed alien
- ☐ Pinocchio
- ☐ Radio
- ☐ Rapunzel
- ☐ Sailor
- ☐ Scarecrow
- ☐ Shark
- ☐ Tarzan
- ☐ Unicorn

Detective Donald kept searching and searching for clues. Next he found himself...

...in an army camp during basic training. Some soldiers were having fun, but most were happy when training was over. Detective Donald noticed a movie camera. Hmmm, he wondered, haven't I seen one somewhere before?

DETECT DONALD AT FORT KNOCKS AND...

- ☐ Ape
- ☐ Bat
- ☐ Bird
- ☐ Bodiless ghost
- ☐ Bombs (2)
- ☐ Cactus
- ☐ Chimneys (2)
- ☐ Cook
- ☐ Dunce cap
- ☐ Fan
- ☐ Fish (2)
- ☐ Jack-o'-lantern
- ☐ Lemonade stand
- ☐ Kite
- ☐ Medal
- ☐ Oil can
- ☐ Periscope
- ☐ Pitcher
- ☐ Pot
- ☐ Rat
- ☐ Robin Hood
- ☐ Sergeant's stripes (5)
- ☐ Skulls (2)
- ☐ Slingshot
- ☐ Snake
- ☐ Sock
- ☐ Traffic ticket
- ☐ Turtle
- ☐ Volcano

Donald walked past the chow line and into...

...the Roman Coliseum. But it wasn't a ruin! It was full of ancient Romans rooting for or against gladiators.

DETECT DONALD IN ANCIENT ROME AND...

- ☐ Abraham Lincoln
- ☐ Banana peel
- ☐ Bones (2)
- ☐ Boots
- ☐ Cheerleader
- ☐ Cleopatra
- ☐ Dog
- ☐ Dragons (2)
- ☐ Electric fan
- ☐ Elephant
- ☐ Football
- ☐ Giraffe
- ☐ Guitar
- ☐ Hot dog
- ☐ Hourglass
- ☐ Jester
- ☐ Kite
- ☐ Lions (3)
- ☐ Lunch boxes (2)
- ☐ Necktie
- ☐ Net
- ☐ Pig
- ☐ Raindrops (2)
- ☐ Red scarf
- ☐ Secret door
- ☐ Soccer ball
- ☐ Spears (2)
- ☐ Tin man
- ☐ Vendors (2)
- ☐ Watch
- ☐ Watering can

Detective Donald ducked out behind the big wooden horse and immediately ran into...

...a wooly mammoth! It was huge and hairy, but how did it get here? Or, how did *he* get *there*? The spear-carrying cave people frightened Detective Donald so he leapt out of their way.

DETECT DONALD IN PREHISTORIC TIMES AND...

- ☐ Ape
- ☐ Arrow
- ☐ Baby bird
- ☐ Basketball
- ☐ Bicycle
- ☐ Bone
- ☐ Book
- ☐ Burglar
- ☐ Cannon
- ☐ Chef
- ☐ Clipboard
- ☐ Helmet
- ☐ Juggler
- ☐ Kettle
- ☐ Mailbox
- ☐ Nets (2)
- ☐ Periscope
- ☐ Pole-vaulter
- ☐ Rabbit
- ☐ Rocket
- ☐ Rocking chair
- ☐ Rocking horse
- ☐ Roller skates
- ☐ Skateboard
- ☐ Skier
- ☐ Tennis racket
- ☐ Toothbrush
- ☐ Tuba
- ☐ Turtle
- ☐ Umbrella
- ☐ Witch

Donald continued on until he came to the back of a curtain. He opened it in time to hear...

..."And now..." He was standing on a stage receiving an award! But why? Then a very embarrassed Detective Donald realized that, without knowing it, he had just walked through ten movie sets!

DETECT DONALD AT THE ACADEMY AWARDS AND...

☐ Aliens (2)
☐ Arrows (2)
☐ Baseball cap
☐ Bird
☐ "Boo" (2)
☐ Bowling ball
☐ Broken heart
☐ Candle
☐ Cook
☐ Darts (5)
☐ Dog
☐ Elephant
☐ Envelope
☐ Fish
☐ Flower
☐ Fork
☐ Ghost
☐ Half moon
☐ Heart
☐ Ice skates
☐ Lens cap
☐ Masks (2)
☐ Microphone
☐ Mushroom
☐ Pencil
☐ Rabbit
☐ Scarf
☐ Skulls (2)
☐ Snake
☐ Tomahawk

LOOK FOR LAURA   DETECT DONALD   FIND FRANKIE   SEARCH FOR SUSIE

WHERE ARE THEY?

FIND FRANKIE

It is the night of the Monster Club meeting. Every monster member, young and old, ugly and uglier is in attendance. The clubhouse is to be torn down and the monsters need a new place to meet. All the monsters are listening carefully—except Frankie.

FIND FRANKIE AT THE MONSTER CLUB MEETING AND...

☐ Arrow
☐ Ax
☐ Balloon
☐ Bats (4)
☐ Birdcage
☐ Bones (4)
☐ Broom
☐ Candles (7)
☐ Candy canes (2)
☐ Clothesline
☐ Cobweb
☐ Coffins (2)
☐ Cup
☐ Grapes
☐ Hot dog
☐ Jack-o'-lantern
☐ Mice (3)
☐ Nail
☐ Noose
☐ Pie
☐ Rabbit
☐ Skulls (4)
☐ Teddy bear
☐ TV set
☐ Voodoo doll
☐ Yo-yo

Suddenly...

...Frankie is lost in the outside world! There are so many sights and sounds, and so much to see. Maybe he can find a new meeting place for the monsters.

FIND FRANKIE ON THE STREET AND...

☐ Alien
☐ Bird singing
☐ Bowling ball
☐ Cat
☐ Elephant
☐ Falling flowerpot
☐ Fire hydrants (3)
☐ Flower van
☐ Football
☐ Guitar
☐ Hamburger
☐ Humpty Dumpty
☐ Karate bird
☐ King
☐ Kite
☐ Monkey
☐ Moose
☐ Mummy
☐ Ostrich
☐ Pizza
☐ Pogo stick
☐ Quicksand
☐ Rocket
☐ Santa Claus
☐ Scarecrow
☐ Tennis player
☐ Toothbrush
☐ Tuba
☐ Turtle
☐ Viking
☐ Water-skier

Frankie wonders where he should go first.

Wow! There's a lot going on in this store! Frankie can easily get lost in this dizzy, busy place.

FIND FRANKIE IN THE SUPER SUPERMARKET AND...

- ☐ Banana peel
- ☐ Basketball
- ☐ Bird
- ☐ Boat
- ☐ Bone
- ☐ Cactus
- ☐ Candles (2)
- ☐ Carrots
- ☐ Cheerleader
- ☐ Clown
- ☐ Duck
- ☐ Elephant
- ☐ "Fido"
- ☐ Fish heads
- ☐ Hammock
- ☐ Igloo
- ☐ Jack-o'-lantern
- ☐ Marshmallow
- ☐ Mermaid
- ☐ Mouse
- ☐ Periscope
- ☐ Ping-Pong ball
- ☐ Roller skates
- ☐ Six other monsters
- ☐ Skull
- ☐ Snowman
- ☐ Surfer
- ☐ Thief
- ☐ Tin Man
- ☐ Toast
- ☐ Wagon
- ☐ Witch
- ☐ Yo-yo

After all this activity, Frankie needs to find a quiet, dark place to relax.

Unfortunately, this show is so bad that even a nice monster like Frankie can't watch it for long.

FIND FRANKIE AT THE THEATER AND...

☐ Alligator
☐ Arrows (2)
☐ Camel
☐ Candle
☐ Chicken
☐ Clipboard
☐ Cowboy
☐ Deer
☐ Elephants (3)
☐ Fire hydrant
☐ Fish (4)
☐ Frog
☐ Ghosts (3)
☐ Giraffe
☐ Hammer
☐ Jack-in-the-box
☐ Jack-o'-lantern
☐ Lost shoe
☐ Mice (3)
☐ Octopus
☐ Paintbrush
☐ Peter Pan
☐ Pillow
☐ Satellite dish
☐ Snail
☐ Star
☐ Tin Man
☐ TV set
☐ Umbrellas (2)

Frankie needs some fresh air. So it's off to...

...a place where the creatures look even stranger than he does. Some have fur and some have feathers. Some have horns. Some are scary!

FIND FRANKIE AT THE ZOO AND...

- ☐ Baby taking a bath
- ☐ Balloons (6)
- ☐ Beach balls (3)
- ☐ Books (2)
- ☐ Brooms (2)
- ☐ Cactus
- ☐ Camera
- ☐ Cowboy
- ☐ Dunce cap
- ☐ Elf
- ☐ Fisherman
- ☐ Flamingo
- ☐ Ghosts (2)
- ☐ Heart
- ☐ Ice-cream cones (2)
- ☐ Kite
- ☐ Old tire
- ☐ Picnic basket
- ☐ Quarter moon
- ☐ Robin Hood
- ☐ Sailor
- ☐ Santa Claus
- ☐ Skateboard
- ☐ Socks (2)
- ☐ Stepladder
- ☐ Telescope
- ☐ Tick-tack-toe
- ☐ Trash baskets (3)
- ☐ Turtle
- ☐ Witch

After the zoo, Frankie is a little hungry...

...so he goes to look for something to eat. He wonders if they serve his favorite monster mash here. Perhaps this would be a good place for the monsters to meet.

Before he gets lost again...

FIND FRANKIE AT THE YUM-YUM EMPORIUM AND...

☐ Arrow
☐ Birdcage
☐ Bone
☐ Chicken man
☐ Cook
☐ Dogs (3)
☐ Fishing pole
☐ Football
☐ Knight
☐ Mailbox
☐ Manager
☐ Panda
☐ Pirate
☐ Princess
☐ Robot
☐ Rubber duck
☐ Salt shaker
☐ Scuba diver
☐ Sheriff
☐ Skulls (2)
☐ Space creature
☐ Star
☐ Straws (2)
☐ Sunglasses (2)
☐ Tombstone
☐ Tray of pizza
☐ Tuba
☐ Turtles (2)
☐ Volcano
☐ Wig

After lunch, Frankie wanders into the aquarium to see some underwater monsters. Even though they're all wet, they seem to be having a good time.

FIND FRANKIE IN THE AQUARIUM AND...

- ☐ Boat
- ☐ Bucket
- ☐ Cans of tuna
- ☐ Cat
- ☑ Diver
- ☐ Dog
- ☐ Duck
- ☐ Ear
- ☐ Eyeglasses
- ☐ Fisherman
- ☐ Flying fish
- ☐ Guitar
- ☐ Hammer
- ☐ Hearts (4)
- ☐ Ice skater
- ☐ Igloo
- ☐ Life preserver
- ☐ Mermaid
- ☐ Magnifying glass
- ☐ Merman
- ☐ Old-fashioned radio
- ☐ Sea horse
- ☐ Socks (2)
- ☐ Starfish (3)
- ☐ Stingray
- ☐ Submarine
- ☐ Surfer
- ☐ Swordfish (2)
- ☐ Tick-tack-toe
- ☐ Tiger
- ☐ Water leak
- ☐ Wooden leg

After watching the fish frolic, Frankie feels like having some fun too.

Hot dog! It's Frankie's first time on wheels! If only his monster friends could see him now.

FIND FRANKIE AT THE ROWDY ROLLER RINK AND...

- ☐ Apple
- ☐ Artist
- ☐ Basketball
- ☐ Bowling ball
- ☐ Boxer
- ☐ Boy Scout
- ☐ Cave man
- ☐ Centaur
- ☐ Centipede
- ☐ Convict
- ☐ Drum
- ☐ Fire hydrant
- ☐ Fish
- ☐ Ghost
- ☐ Giant roller skate
- ☐ Guitar
- ☐ Half-stop sign
- ☐ Hockey player
- ☐ Ice skater
- ☐ Jugglers (2)
- ☐ Paintbrushes (2)
- ☐ Piano
- ☐ Pillow
- ☐ Scarfs (2)
- ☐ Skier
- ☐ Snow woman
- ☐ Super hero
- ☐ Swan
- ☐ Three-legged skater
- ☐ Unicorn
- ☐ Weight lifter
- ☐ Witch
- ☐ Zebra

After rocking and rolling around the rink, Frankie sees a place with lots of space monsters on video screens. He hears bloops and bleeps, bzaps and bliks—sounds that Frankie's friends usually make.

FIND FRANKIE IN THE ARCADE AND...

☐ Angel
☐ Baseball
☐ Bat
☐ Bathtub
☐ Bomb
☐ Bottle
☐ Bow
☐ Carrot
☐ Darts (4)
☐ Dog
☐ Earmuffs
☐ Giraffe
☐ Hammer
☐ Headless player
☐ Heart
☐ Highest score
☐ Horseshoe
☐ Ice-cream cone
☐ Jack-o'-lantern
☐ Painter
☐ Paper airplane
☐ Pillow
☐ Pinocchio
☐ Rabbit
☐ Robot
☐ Snakes (5)
☐ Spinning top
☐ Surfer
☐ Traffic ticket
☐ Trash can
☐ Wrecking ball

All the noise makes Frankie want to look for a peaceful place...

...outside of the city. This seems like a great place to live. If only he can find a nice, ugly home where the monsters can meet.

FIND FRANKIE IN THE SUBURBS AND...

- ☐ Badminton game
- ☐ Bird
- ☐ Caddy
- ☐ Candle
- ☐ Clown
- ☐ Cow
- ☐ Dogs (3)
- ☐ Duck
- ☐ Fencing star
- ☐ Fire hydrants (4)
- ☐ Flat tire
- ☐ Footballs (2)
- ☐ Hearts (3)
- ☐ Hose
- ☐ Hot dog mobile
- ☐ Ice-cream cone
- ☐ Ice skate
- ☐ Kite
- ☐ Lion
- ☐ Marching band
- ☐ Paper delivery
- ☐ Photographer
- ☐ Pig
- ☐ Pyramid
- ☐ Shark
- ☐ Telescope
- ☐ Treasure chest
- ☐ Tepee
- ☐ Umbrella
- ☐ Unicorn
- ☐ Unicycle
- ☐ Zebra

Wait! Maybe there is a place! Can you see it?

There, at the top of the hill, Frankie finds the perfect meeting house. The monsters finally find Frankie and elect him President of the Monster Club. What a great time for a party!

FIND FRANKIE AT THE MONSTERS' NEW CLUBHOUSE AND...

- ☐ Bats (4)
- ☐ Bones (4)
- ☐ Bottle
- ☐ Candles (2)
- ☐ Clock
- ☐ Coffeepot
- ☐ Coffin
- ☐ Cup
- ☐ Dog
- ☐ Flower
- ☐ Flying carpet
- ☐ Football
- ☐ Ghosts (5)
- ☐ Happy star
- ☐ Headless man
- ☐ Light bulb
- ☐ Mail carrier
- ☐ Mouse
- ☐ Mummy
- ☐ Octopus
- ☐ Pencil sharpener
- ☐ Skulls (4)
- ☐ Sled
- ☐ Snake
- ☐ Sword
- ☐ Tick-tack-toe
- ☐ Tombstones (2)
- ☐ Thirteens (4)
- ☐ Three-headed
      monster
- ☐ Top hat
- ☐ TV set
- ☐ Two-headed monster
- ☐ Umbrella
- ☐ Witch

FIND FRANKIE   SEARCH FOR SUSIE   LOOK FOR LAURA   DETECT DONALD

WHERE ARE THEY?

LOOK FOR LAURA

Laura lives on a planet called MAXX. One day she decided to visit her grandmother in her astro-ferry. All her friends came to say good-bye.

LOOK FOR LAURA ON THE PLANET MAXX AND...

- ☐ Balloons (3)
- ☐ Birdhouse
- ☐ Birds (2)
- ☐ Books (3)
- ☐ Clipboard
- ☐ Clocks (4)
- ☐ Coffeepot
- ☐ Covered wagon
- ☐ Dog
- ☐ Elephant
- ☐ Evergreen tree
- ☐ Fish
- ☐ Flowerpot
- ☐ Footballs (2)
- ☐ Fork
- ☐ Graduate
- ☐ Hamburger
- ☐ Hot dog
- ☐ Ice-cream pop
- ☐ Jump rope
- ☐ Kite
- ☐ Old radio
- ☐ Old tire
- ☐ Pizza
- ☐ Sled
- ☐ Tepee
- ☐ Train engine
- ☐ Turtle
- ☐ TV set
- ☐ Umbrella

But when Laura got into the astro-ferry, she pressed the wrong button.

Suddenly she was in an alien world surrounded by strange-looking creatures. Everything was wet! This wasn't her grandmother's house. This wasn't MAXX. This wasn't even land!

LOOK FOR LAURA IN THE OCEAN AND...

- ☐ Anchovy
- ☐ Bats (2)
- ☐ Bell
- ☐ Books (2)
- ☐ Bow
- ☐ Cheese
- ☐ Crown
- ☐ Cup
- ☐ Fire hydrant
- ☐ Flowers (2)
- ☐ Ghost
- ☐ Guitar
- ☐ Hammer
- ☐ Haystack
- ☐ Heart
- ☐ Horseshoe
- ☐ Ice-cream cone
- ☐ Key
- ☐ Mermaid
- ☐ Needlefish
- ☐ Octopus
- ☐ Old tire
- ☐ Pencil
- ☐ Pizza
- ☐ Saw
- ☐ Seesaw
- ☐ Snail
- ☐ Straw hat
- ☐ Telescope
- ☐ Treasure chest
- ☐ Turtles (3)
- ☐ TV set
- ☐ Umbrella

Laura zoomed up and finally landed...

...in a jungle watering hole. There the creatures were furry and feathery.

LOOK FOR LAURA AT THE WATERING HOLE AND...

- Arrow
- Balloons (3)
- Beach ball
- Birdbath
- Bird's nest
- Boat
- Bones (3)
- Camel
- Camera
- Crocodile
- Donkey
- Feather
- Football
- Giraffe
- Heart
- Jack-o'-lantern
- Joe of the jungle
- Lion
- Lollipop
- Owl
- Pelican
- Periscope
- Pig
- Rooster
- Snake
- Socks (2)
- Tin can
- Toucan
- Unicorn
- Wart hog
- Wolf
- Worm
- Yo-yo

But Laura wasn't sure if they were all friendly, so she got back on board and decided to explore the rest of this strange world.

As Laura flew through the sky, she saw some mountains covered with white stuff. Laura landed and for the very first time she saw— SNOW! This was fun! She wished her friends on MAXX could see the snow too.

LOOK FOR LAURA ON A SKI SLOPE IN THE ALPS AND...

☐ Alligator
☐ Artist
☐ Automobile
☐ Boat
☐ Bone
☐ Bunny
☐ Camel
☐ Cold telephone
☐ Dog
☐ Elf
☐ Evergreen tree
☐ Fish
☐ Football player
☐ Hammock
☐ Igloo
☐ Jack-o'-lantern
☐ Kite
☐ Mailbox
☐ Mouse
☐ Rake
☐ Santa Claus
☐ Scuba diver
☐ Skateboard
☐ Sleeping monster
☐ Snowman
☐ Sunglasses
☐ Top hat
☐ Turtle
☐ TV antenna
☐ Uphill skier

Then she was frightened by a loud yodel and away she went.

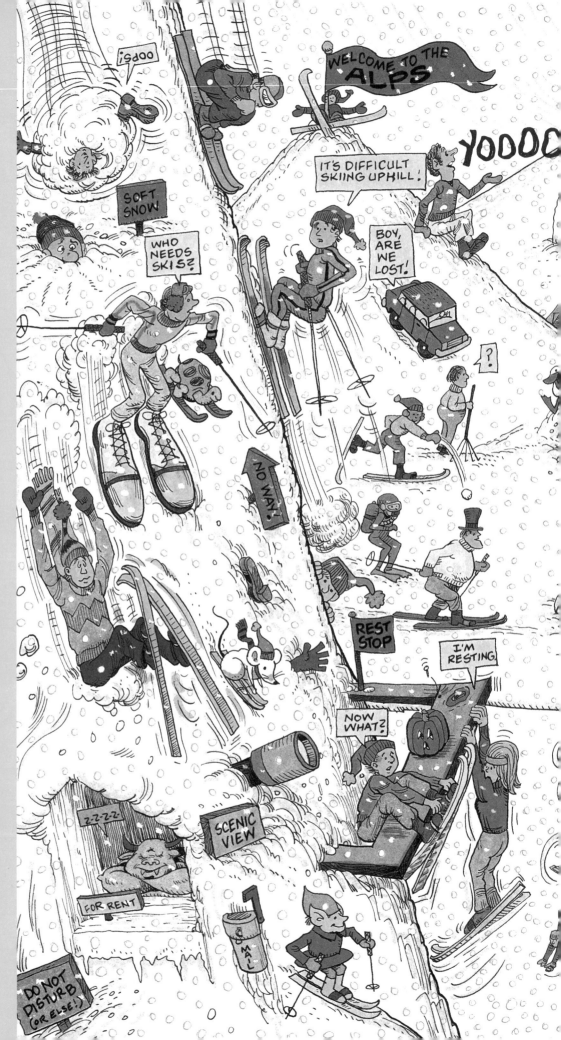

Laura flew south and landed in the desert—or rather, an oasis in the desert. Wow, it was hot! And people had towels on their heads! Everyone was too busy buying and selling at the bazaar to notice Laura, so she continued on her journey.

LOOK FOR LAURA AT THE BAH-HA BAZAAR AND...

- ☐ Beach ball
- ☐ Bird
- ☐ Broom
- ☐ Cat
- ☐ Clouds (2)
- ☐ Coconuts (4)
- ☐ Dog
- ☐ Donkey
- ☐ Elephant
- ☐ Flying carpets (2)
- ☐ Football
- ☐ Genie
- ☐ Horn
- ☐ Ice-cream cone
- ☐ Igloo
- ☐ Kite
- ☐ Necklace
- ☐ Oil well
- ☐ Pillow fight
- ☐ Rabbit
- ☐ Shovel
- ☐ Skier
- ☐ Sled
- ☐ Snail
- ☐ Snakes (4)
- ☐ Straw baskets (2)
- ☐ Sunglasses
- ☐ Telescope
- ☐ Tents (4)
- ☐ Truck
- ☐ Turtle
- ☐ Umbrella

Back north went the astro-ferry. Laura saw many beautiful places as she flew over Europe, so she decided to visit them.

LOOK FOR LAURA IN EUROPE AND...

☐ Automobiles (2)
☐ Ball
☐ Ballerinas (2)
☐ Boats (3)
☐ Cancan dancers
☐ Castle
☐ Dog
☐ Donkey
☐ Egret
☐ Fisherman
☐ Flying fish
☐ Ghost
☐ Gondola
☐ Hot-air balloon
☐ King
☐ Knight in armor
☐ Non-flying fish (3)
☐ Periscope
☐ Reindeer
☐ Skier
☐ Snake
☐ Snowmen (2)
☐ Starfish
☐ Stork
☐ Telescope
☐ Tour bus
☐ Train
☐ Tulips
☐ Turtle
☐ Windmill

Laura was beginning to get homesick and she wondered how she would find her way back to MAXX.

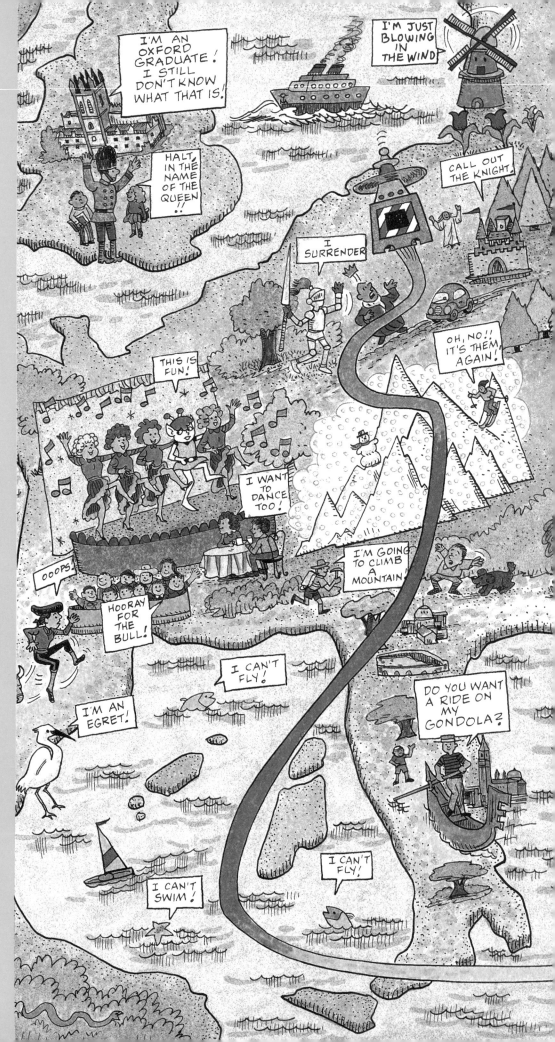

From the astro-ferry, Laura spotted a large group of children doing different activities. Maybe they could help.

LOOK FOR LAURA AT SUMMER CAMP AND...

☐ Alligator
☐ Basket
☐ Bats (2)
☐ Bear
☐ Broom
☐ Candy cane
☐ Cannon
☐ Cheese
☐ Cooks (2)
☐ Duck
☐ Firefighter
☐ Fish
☐ Head of a monster
☐ Headless monster
☐ Jack-o'-lantern
☐ Lake
☐ Lamp
☐ Motorcycle
☐ Owl
☐ Paper airplane
☐ Pizza
☐ Scarecrow
☐ Shovel
☐ Skateboard
☐ Skulls (2)
☐ Stepladder
☐ Target
☐ Telephone
☐ Three-legged chair
☐ Tin can
☐ Toy duck
☐ Wagon
☐ Witch

Laura had never seen so many strange activities. And no one had ever heard of the planet, MAXX.

The kids at camp directed Laura to a huge tent down the road. In the center of the tent, silly people, and animals too, seemed to be having fun.

LOOK FOR LAURA AT THE CIRCUS AND...

- ☐ Bad juggler
- ☐ Banana peel
- ☐ Binoculars
- ☐ Bowling ball
- ☐ Bow tie
- ☐ Cactus
- ☐ Cheese
- ☐ Cowboy hats (2)
- ☐ Dry paint
- ☐ Elephants (2)
- ☐ Ghost
- ☐ Hot dog
- ☐ Ice-cream cone
- ☐ Knight in armor
- ☐ Lion
- ☐ Lost shoe
- ☐ Monkey suit
- ☐ Mouse
- ☐ Picture frame
- ☐ Pie
- ☐ Pig
- ☐ Pirate
- ☐ Shoe shine box
- ☐ Skateboards (3)
- ☐ Top hat
- ☐ Training wheels
- ☐ Umbrella
- ☐ Walking flower
- ☐ Watering can

Laura enjoyed herself at the circus, but she was worried about getting home.

She tried again to get the astro-ferry to head for MAXX. Instead, she landed in a noisy city. Laura was about to give up hope of ever returning home. Then she saw some beings that looked a little like herself.

LOOK FOR LAURA IN WASHINGTON D.C. AND...

- ☐ Artist
- ☐ Birds (2)
- ☐ Bones (3)
- ☐ Books (3)
- ☐ Bows (4)
- ☐ Brush
- ☐ Camera
- ☐ Campaign poster
- ☐ Cat
- ☐ Envelope
- ☐ Goose
- ☐ Hammer
- ☐ Hard hats (2)
- ☐ Hot-air balloon
- ☐ Jogger
- ☐ Kangaroo
- ☐ Kite
- ☐ Magnifying glass
- ☐ Pentagon
- ☐ "People Working"
- ☐ Sailor's hat
- ☐ Scarecrow
- ☐ Secret agent
- ☐ Sleeping man
- ☐ Toolbox
- ☐ Turtle
- ☐ Tyrannosaurus
- ☐ Wagon
- ☐ Washington Monument

Perhaps they could help her, so she followed them as they walked...

...back to school! In the classroom, Laura watched the children do their spelling lessons. H-O-M-E spelled home.

LOOK FOR LAURA AT SCHOOL AND...

- ☐ Alexander
- ☐ Bat
- ☐ Bells (2)
- ☐ Broom
- ☐ Bubble gum
- ☐ Cat
- ☐ Clothespin
- ☐ Cupcake
- ☐ Drummer
- ☐ Easel
- ☐ Fish (2)
- ☐ Footballs (2)
- ☐ Globe
- ☐ Golf club
- ☐ Half moon
- ☐ Happy face
- ☐ Hats (2)
- ☐ Heart
- ☐ Hourglass
- ☐ Igloo
- ☐ Jump rope
- ☐ Monster mask
- ☐ Owl
- ☐ Paintbrush
- ☐ Pinocchio
- ☐ Plate
- ☐ Protoceratops
- ☐ Robin
- ☐ Robot
- ☐ School bags (2)
- ☐ Scissors
- ☐ Snow
- ☐ Soccer ball
- ☐ Stocking
- ☐ Sunglasses
- ☐ Wastepaper basket

Suddenly, Laura decided to type "M-A-X-X" in the astro-ferry's computer.

It worked! The astro-ferry zoomed home! Everyone was gathered to welcome her back to MAXX. Laura told them all about the many strange and wonderful things she had seen on Earth.

LOOK FOR LAURA AT THE WELCOME HOME PARTY AND...

☐ Alien-in-the-box
☐ Baseball cap
☐ Basket
☐ Bone
☐ Candle
☐ Carrot
☐ Cheese
☐ Cupcake
☐ Evergreen tree
☐ Falling stars (7)
☐ Fire hydrant
☐ Football
☐ Graduate
☐ Guitar
☐ Hamburger
☐ Hammer
☐ Hot dog
☐ Ice-cream soda
☐ Light bulb
☐ Meatball
☐ Mouse
☐ Pencils (2)
☐ Rose
☐ Screwdriver
☐ Shovel
☐ Snail
☐ Tent
☐ Turtle
☐ TV set
☐ Unicorn
☐ Yo-yo

From now on, Laura will be very careful when she travels in her astro-ferry.

DETECT DONALD   FIND FRANKIE   SEARCH FOR SUSIE   LOOK FOR LAURA

WHERE ARE THEY?

SEARCH FOR SUSIE

One day Susie's mom and dad took her to the Big Fun Amusement Park. Susie was excited and couldn't wait to see all the rides. While her parents were buying popcorn, Susie wandered off and started to explore the park.

SEARCH FOR SUSIE IN THE BIG FUN PARK AND...

☐ Banana peel
☐ Bowling ball
☐ Burst balloon
☐ Camel
☐ Candle
☐ Clothesline
☐ Clown-o-saurus (3)
☐ Ducks (2)
☐ Ear of corn
☐ Egg
☐ Football
☐ Ghost
☐ Hearts (2)
☐ Ice-cream cone
☐ Jack-o'-lantern
☐ Juggler
☐ Magnifying glass
☐ Megaphone
☐ Octopus
☐ Pencil
☐ Periscopes (2)
☐ Police (6)
☐ Raccoon
☐ Red wagon
☐ Reindeer
☐ Socks (2)
☐ Sour-puss-saurus
☐ Turtle
☐ Violinist

"Where's Susie?" asked her father.

"I don't know," answered her mother. "But we'd better start looking for her."

Meanwhile, Susie heard lots of shouting and splashing. Everyone seemed to be having fun. Or were they?

SEARCH FOR SUSIE AT THE WATER RIDE AND...

- ☐ Bone
- ☐ Bride
- ☐ Cactus
- ☐ Candy canes (2)
- ☐ Cupcake
- ☐ Curtains
- ☐ Dogs (2)
- ☐ Egg
- ☐ Fire hydrant
- ☐ Fish (4)
- ☐ Flying horse
- ☐ Goat
- ☐ Ground hog
- ☐ Hearts (3)
- ☐ Hobbyhorse
- ☐ Hot dog
- ☐ Island
- ☐ Moby Dick
- ☐ Nightmare
- ☐ Peter Pan
- ☐ Pickle barrel
- ☐ Police-o-saurus
- ☐ Sailboat
- ☐ Sea horse
- ☐ Surfboard
- ☐ Tuba
- ☐ Umbrella

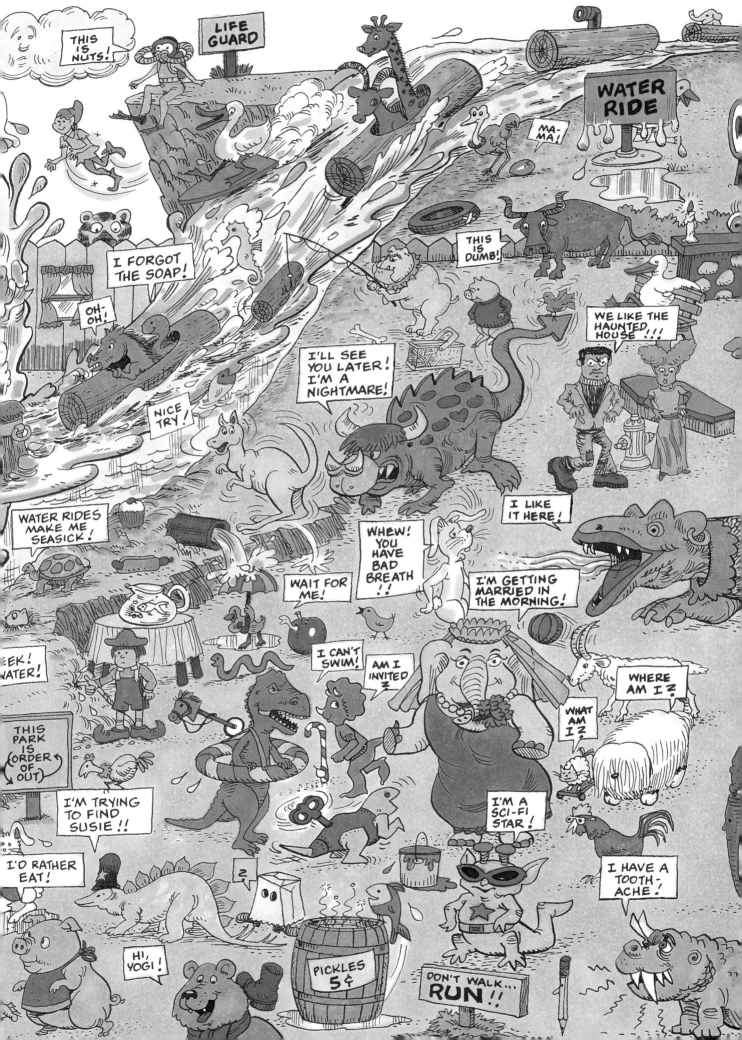

Susie left the Water Ride and headed for the carousel. Around and around it went. Susie thought she heard her parents calling her, but with all the noise and excitement she couldn't find them.

SEARCH FOR SUSIE AT THE CAROUSEL AND...

☐ Alarm clock
☐ Ball
☐ Bat
☐ Broom
☐ Butterfly
☐ Cannon
☐ Dancing bears (2)
☐ Dentist
☐ Ear
☐ Fan
☐ Frog
☐ Golf bag
☐ Kangaroo
☐ Lamp
☐ Lollipop
☐ Mushroom
☐ Neckties (3)
☐ Parrot
☐ Pig
☐ Roller skate
☐ Scarecrow
☐ Snake
☐ Snow lady
☐ Super hero
☐ Telescope
☐ Top hat
☐ Truck
☐ Turtles (2)
☐ Unicorn
☐ Yo-yo

Susie's next stop was the Fun House. Wow! Things were really wild in there! Susie's mom and dad were searching for her in the Fun House too.

SEARCH FOR SUSIE IN THE FUN HOUSE AND...

- ☐ Banana peel
- ☐ Barrel
- ☐ Bib
- ☐ Cave man
- ☐ Cup
- ☐ Football helmet
- ☐ Headless body
- ☐ Humpty Dumpty
- ☐ Igloo
- ☐ Jack-in-a-box
- ☐ Jack-o'-lantern
- ☐ Kite
- ☐ Magician
- ☐ Medal
- ☐ Parachute
- ☐ Pie
- ☐ Pillow
- ☐ Pot
- ☐ Puppy
- ☐ Saw
- ☐ Sled
- ☐ Snake
- ☐ Sock
- ☐ Stool
- ☐ Susie's parents
- ☐ Target
- ☐ Traffic light
- ☐ Train engine
- ☐ Wacky clock
- ☐ Watermelon slice
- ☐ Wreath

Susie finally found her way through the maze and out of the Fun House. Then she heard loud, squeaking sounds which she followed to a huge, spinning Ferris wheel. "What a neat park this is," thought Susie.

SEARCH FOR SUSIE AT THE FERRIS WHEEL AND...

- ☐ Arrow
- ☐ Astronaut
- ☐ Birdhouse
- ☐ Broom
- ☐ Camera
- ☐ Candy cane
- ☐ Chimney
- ☐ Copycat
- ☐ Dinosaur guitarist
- ☐ Eye
- ☐ Golfer
- ☐ Hammock
- ☐ Hockey stick
- ☐ Ice skates
- ☐ Kite
- ☐ Lions (2)
- ☐ Oil can
- ☐ "Oup and Doup"
- ☐ Painters (2)
- ☐ Papa bear
- ☐ Plumber's plunger
- ☐ Santa Claus
- ☐ Screw
- ☐ Star
- ☐ Surfer
- ☐ Susie's parents
- ☐ Telephone
- ☐ Ticket collector
- ☐ Umbrella
- ☐ Watering can

Susie couldn't resist a ride on a roller coaster. Even an old, rickety-looking roller coaster. She bought a ticket and off she went!

SEARCH FOR SUSIE ON THE ROCK AND ROLLER COASTER RIDE AND...

☐ Balloons (5)
☐ Bat
☐ Birdcage
☐ Boat
☐ Can
☐ Carrot
☐ Cave man
☐ Dino-in-a-bottle
☐ Drummer
☐ Firefighter
☐ Fire hydrant
☐ Flames
☐ Flower eater
☐ Mailbox
☐ Moose
☐ Mummy
☐ Police-o-saurus
☐ Rabbits (5)
☐ Red tire
☐ Rocket
☐ Safe
☐ Skateboard
☐ Skier
☐ Sock
☐ Tennis racket
☐ Tick-tack-toe
☐ Unicycle
☐ Weights
☐ Window
☐ Wreath

Meanwhile, Susie's parents were still searching for her.

After a thrilling ride on the roller coaster, Susie needed a nice, quiet place to relax. The Game Room seemed like the perfect spot. Not much was happening there.

SEARCH FOR SUSIE IN THE GAME ROOM AND...

☐ Apples (2)
☐ Baseball
☐ Basketball
☐ Bomb
☐ Boomerang
☐ Can
☐ Candle
☐ Carrot
☐ Coffeepot
☐ Cup
☐ Dice
☐ Donkey's tail
☐ Dracula
☐ Earmuffs
☐ Ghost
☐ Gift box
☐ Graduate
☐ Guitar
☐ Hammer
☐ Horseshoe
☐ Pencil
☐ Poodle
☐ Sailboat
☐ Telescope
☐ Timekeeper
☐ Top hat
☐ Turtles (3)
☐ Umpire
☐ Unicorn
☐ Yo-yo

Susie played a few games, then headed for...

...the bumper cars! What an exciting ride that was! Susie banged and bumped and crashed her way from one end to the other. She waved to her parents who unfortunately got bumped before they could see her.

SEARCH FOR SUSIE ON THE BUMPER CARS AND...

- [ ] Alien
- [ ] Artist
- [ ] Banana peel
- [ ] Birdcage
- [ ] Bride
- [ ] Cactus
- [ ] Camel
- [ ] Candy cane
- [ ] Cans (5)
- [ ] Car "007"
- [ ] Car "8A"
- [ ] Car "54"
- [ ] Cat
- [ ] Crown
- [ ] Fire hydrant
- [ ] Giraffes (2)
- [ ] Hot dog
- [ ] Ice-cream cone
- [ ] Jack-o'-lantern
- [ ] Kite
- [ ] Light bulb
- [ ] Mice (2)
- [ ] Musician
- [ ] Pig
- [ ] Police (2)
- [ ] Shoemobile
- [ ] Speed limit
- [ ] Stars (2)
- [ ] Sunglasses
- [ ] Surfer
- [ ] Target

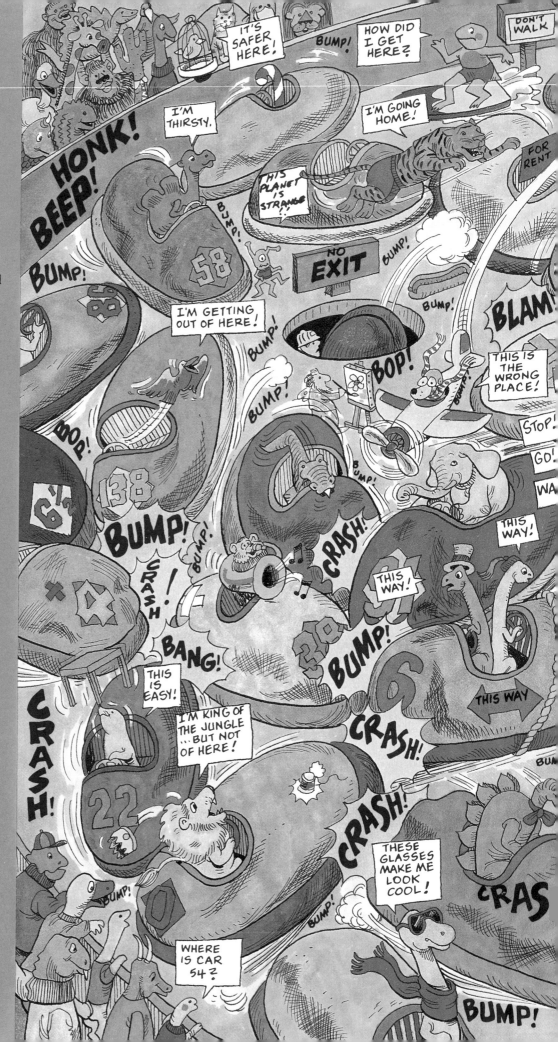

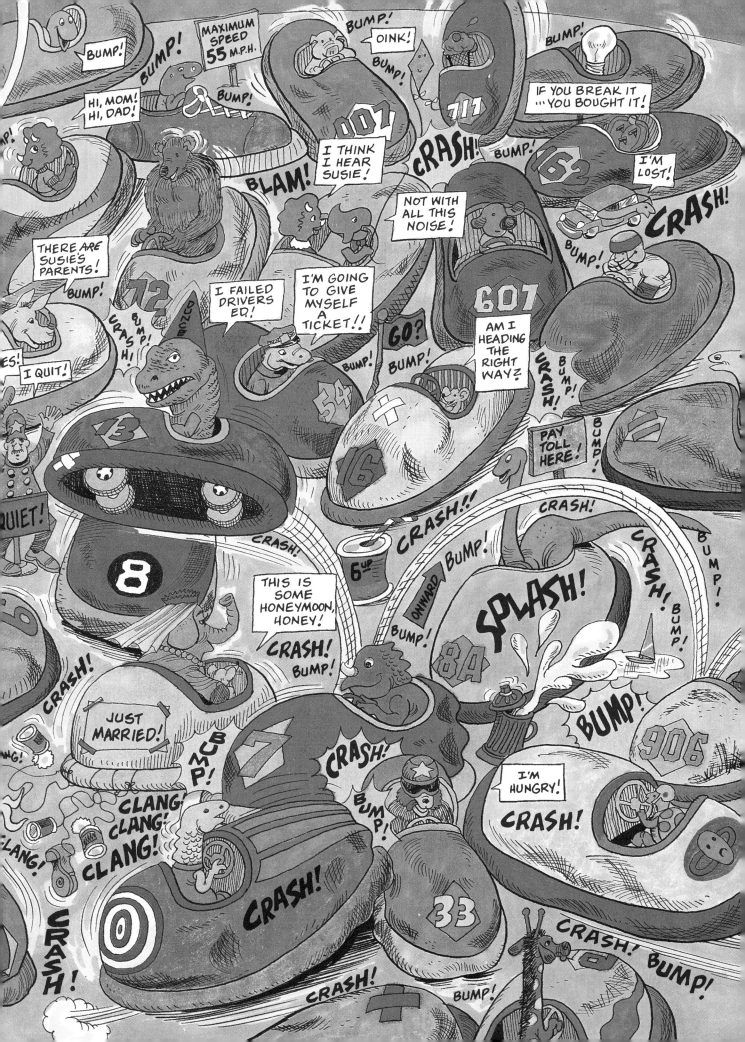

After a long day of fun, Susie was getting hungry. She wondered where she might find a delicious banana split. Then Susie spotted a giant ice-cream cone.

SEARCH FOR SUSIE AT THE ICE-CREAM SHOP AND...

☐ Bad-news lizard
☐ Balloons (3)
☐ Clock
☐ Drum
☐ Eyeglasses
☐ Fish
☐ Fudge pop
☐ Igloo
☐ Kangaroo
☐ King Kong
☐ Mushroom
☐ Paint bucket
☐ Santa Claus
☐ Sled
☐ Slice of pie
☐ Snail
☐ Socks (2)
☐ Sombrero
☐ Spoon
☐ Teeth
☐ Telescope
☐ Tepee
☐ Tire
☐ Top hat
☐ Toy duck
☐ Toy train
☐ TV set
☐ Umbrella
☐ Unicorn

Mom and Dad were still searching and searching for Susie. And...

...there she was! On the giant swings! Susie couldn't wait to tell them about all the fun she had in the Big Fun Amusement Park.

SEARCH FOR SUSIE ON THE GIANT SWINGS AND...

- ☐ Bat
- ☐ Bell
- ☐ Birdhouse
- ☐ Blue sneaker
- ☐ Bone
- ☐ Broken ropes (3)
- ☐ Broom
- ☐ Bucket of red paint
- ☐ Candle
- ☐ Car
- ☐ Carrot
- ☐ Chickens (2)
- ☐ Fish
- ☐ Football
- ☐ Fork
- ☐ Genie
- ☐ Horn
- ☐ Human acrobats (2)
- ☐ Ice-cream cone
- ☐ Ice skate
- ☐ Magnifying glass
- ☐ Paper airplane
- ☐ Parachute
- ☐ Scissors
- ☐ Slingshot
- ☐ Snake
- ☐ Soccer ball
- ☐ Stars (4)
- ☐ Ticket collector
- ☐ Top hat
- ☐ Waiter
- ☐ Wrecking ball

SEARCH FOR SUSIE   LOOK FOR LAURA   DETECT DONALD   FIND FRANKIE